WHY THIS FIGHT?

CONTENTS

Why This Fight?

KISHA CAMPBELL

SUPERIOR WORKS
PUBLISHING

INTRODUCTION

Ephesians 6:12 ERV Our fight is not against people on earth. We are fighting against the rulers and authorities and the powers of this world's darkness. We are fighting against the spiritual powers of evil in the heavenly places.

The chapters in this book you're about to read are about some of the most painful times of my life, and a few of the women who are very important to me. I share their stories of what they endured with the loss of their sons.

To be honest, I do not know where I would be without God. My life, coming into this world in 1977, wasn't easy. The challenges I faced as an infant and now, with added obstacles as an adult, have been nothing short of painful experiences. While I don't want to glorify the pain, I'm writing this book to help "you" understand how God has taken my pain and made it work for my good.

You see, pain is an indicator.

Most of us know how vehicles operate, and every car has an indicator to signal a potential problem. The same indicator gets turned on with pain. It reflects a problem, situation, or issue that somehow needs attention before the entire body breaks down.

What I want you to get out of this book is a greater understanding of how important it is to process your pain and how much more you can grow by dealing with it. YES, I said that! Your pain is purposeful, and your pain will produce growth! If I hadn't gone through all that I've been through, my God, my life at this very moment in time would probably be nonexistent. God has a funny sense of humor. When you ask Him to pump the brakes on your life, it suddenly starts moving in a progressive direction.

Life can be very painful, and the Lord knows my life has had a ton of pain. Like a long, winding road filled with potholes. But once the pages of the book turn, you'll understand what I mean by making your pain work for you. God has been with me throughout my life journey! Although I've had many painful experiences, I'm grateful to God for guiding me through them all.

On the pages of this book, you will find 'My Truths'!

Happy Reading,

Kisha

| 1 |

The Fight to Live: Why Me, God?

The question "Why me, God?" has likely echoed through human hearts since the beginning of time. It's a question born out of suffering, confusion, and pain. I asked it too. But in return, I heard a different question: "Why not you?"

We seek reasons for our trials and often wonder if they are punishment. But perhaps these challenges point toward purpose. When God allows us into a battle, it's not to break us but to reveal His purpose. The Supreme Creator, in His wisdom, entrusts us with battles not for defeat but for victory. If He has called you into a fight, consider it an honor—He is using you to demonstrate His power. This idea became especially real to me during my own unexpected battle.

Fighting isn't always natural. At times it's spiritual. When a struggle comes, you might feel drained or weak. You question your strength. But God equips us, even when we're unready. Sometimes, we fight not by choice, but necessity—to live. We fight because God already promised victory.

For me, the hardest battle I've faced was breast cancer. I didn't want that fight, but it came anyway. Cancer isn't distant—it's close. Many of us will face it personally or with someone we love. Cancer disrupts the body's natural design, with diseased cells growing uncontrollably where healing and renewal should occur.

The Diagnosis

The day of my diagnosis, we were returning from dropping our youngest off at college. I had a follow-up appointment. Doctors had mentioned a lump before, didn't seem worried, so I expected the usual. But they said, "You have stage 1 breast cancer."

I felt the air leave my lungs. The world slowed. Me? Cancer? I never imagined that would be my fight. Still, there I was. I shared the news with my husband and mom. It felt like a death sentence. I made a plan and changed my diet. After weeks of worry, Stage 1 became Stage 0.

In the months before my diagnosis, I kept noticing the time 4:44. Searching for its meaning brought no answers until later, when I realized 444 symbolized God's protection and presence. When I received my diagnosis, I was four months from my 44th birthday. Even before the battle, God's presence was with me.

I've fought battles all my life: seizures as an infant, years relying on medicine. But cancer felt different. I asked God, "Why would You let me go through this?" and heard, "This is not unto death." Clinging to that promise, I spoke God's word through every appointment and surgery.

Cancer makes you feel you're lost in the wilderness, like even God has forgotten your name. It's a lonely road. And yet, even in the darkest places, God is there. To make sense of this loneliness, I often thought of Job. In Job 1:8 (NKJV), God says: "Then the Lord said to Satan, 'Have you considered My servant Job, that there is none like him on the earth, a blameless and upright man, one who fears God and shuns evil?'"

God was proud of Job. Job suffered. But in Job 1:22 (NKJV): "In all this Job did not sin nor charge God with wrong."
Job's story shows that our battles exist to display God's glory, not as punishment, but as purpose. I reminded myself—this isn't about

me. It's about what God wants to show the world through me. I learned to set aside my emotions and trust Him.

Emerging from this fight, I survived breast cancer. Today, I encourage every woman: get your mammograms. Don't delay or ignore signs. Early detection saved my life, and God healed me.

To the men reading: encourage the women you love—wives, daughters, sisters, friends—to get checked. Your voice may save them.

This is The Fight to Live. By God's grace, I'm still here.

http://www.cancer.gov/about-cancrer/understanding/what-is-cancer

| 2 |

The Fight to Get Rid of the Pain

WHAT IS PAIN?

When I think of pain, I picture the sharpness of a blow to the stomach. Yet, for many, pain goes deeper and can be a source of strength, building resilience. To me, pain is when life doesn't align with our desires.

As a child, I rarely faced raw pain because of my grandmother, Shirley Ann Tinch, and my great-grandmother, Mary "Granny" Greene. They shielded me from life's harshness—Grandma Shirley soothed disappointments before they could take root, while Granny Greene, though firmer, gave steadying love that held me together. These women became my foundation when trouble arose.

Through them, I learned pain isn't just something to escape—it shapes us. Grandma Shirley showed me comfort that fought isolation, while Granny's discipline taught me that pain refines rather than destroys. This realization would later help me understand the broader nature of suffering.

The Webster Dictionary describes pain as "mental or emotional suffering." No two people's pain is the same, and pain tolerance varies. Recognizing this, it's important to understand how each of us responds when pain seeks our attention.

Pain signals something is out of order in your life—a warning light alerting you to pay attention. Whether it's in finances, health, or relationships, pain acts as an internal prompt that calls for action. Responding could mean seeking alignment through self-reflection, counseling, prayer, or honest conversation.

Pain is not always the enemy; often it's your soul signaling a need for change. Treat your pain like a car's warning light and ask: What needs to be adjusted? If your health is suffering, be accountable for what you consume, or see a doctor. If the pain is emotional, the signal might require counseling, prayer, journaling, or open dialogues that free you from pretending everything's fine.

I try not to prescribe how anyone should feel when dealing with pain. I remember feeling stressed at a job while watching others leave for better positions, feeling stuck myself. One day, a colleague noticed my stress and said, "You're making yourself sick by worrying." My struggle to leave that job brought so much stress that I ended up on additional medication. Pain affects both body and mind, and coping with it can be challenging.

I'm a steadfast advocate for both therapy and faith. Combining these has helped me throughout my journey. The path to healing is challenging, and pain can distract you, making it hard to see God's presence and work in your life. Hagar's story is a powerful example. As an Egyptian slave, she endured hardships but remained humble. The Lord met her during one of her most difficult moments. She was drawn into a situation that she and Abraham had not anticipated. Pain led her to run and hide, yet her encounter with God through an angel brought her a promise and reminded her that her suffering was heard. If you ever feel your struggles are small, let Hagar's story encourage you to trust your own path toward healing.

*G*enesis 16:3-10 NIV
3 So after Abram had been living in Canaan ten years, Sarai, his wife, took her Egyptian slave Hagar and gave her to her husband to be his wife. 4 He slept with Hagar, and she conceived.

When she knew she was pregnant, she began to despise her mistress. 5 Then Sarai said to Abram, "You are responsible for the wrong I am suffering. I put my slave in your arms, and now that she knows she is pregnant, she despises me. May the Lord judge between you and me."

6 "Your slave is in your hands," Abram said. "Do with her whatever you think best." Then Sarai mistreated Hagar; so she fled from her.

7 The angel of the Lord found Hagar near a spring in the desert; it was the spring that is beside the road to Shur. 8 And he said, "Hagar, slave of Sarai, where have you come from, and where are you going?"

"I'm running away from my mistress Sarai," she answered.

The angel of the Lord then told her, "Go back to your mistress and be submissive to her." He continued, "I will multiply your descendants so greatly that they will be uncountable."

| 3 |

The Fight for a Relationship with My Father

194-289 THE DC JAIL# THAT WAS GIVEN TO HIM

Mr. Anthony Lorenzo Moten Sr. was born on August 29, 1959, to Mary Evelyn and George Harrison Moten. He was their fourth child. I never really knew how my father's life was when he came into the world. How did his parents meet? What did they dream about, or pray for? His story always felt like it had pieces missing, and he rarely spoke about his past. I believe he kept those pieces to himself, never truly getting to know his own parents. At five years old, he lost his mother. That kind of pain—I can't even imagine. His father, I was told, called him a "momma's boy." With that, the first seed of pain was planted in my father's life.

He didn't grow up with the foundation most of us expect. For him and his siblings, Granny Mary Greene, his grandmother, became their caregiver—a sacrifice born out of love. Yet I often wonder: how did she navigate her grief over losing her only daughter while raising her grandchildren? What my father endured as a child shaped everything he became. When he was 18, an incident led to his imprisonment—a revelation that shocked me. The man I knew was soft-spoken and thoughtful. He faced 75 years in prison, but that wasn't the end of his story. Instead, by the grace of God and with determination, he entered programs that changed the trajectory of his life. These programs opened an unexpected door for early release, one I never imagined would swing open so soon.

When we were younger, my brother Tony and I visited him in Lorton. Hoping to keep us calm, my mother played musical tapes in the car. Still, the ride felt heavy. They called it "school," but my father's school had barbed wire and guards. On those visits, my compassion for people in prison began.

My dad passed away in 2010. I don't think I've ever fully expressed how much I really miss and love him until now. He had gone through so much loss: prison, rejection—and yet, he tried to love us the best way he could. He was very intelligent. I love and miss that part of him a great deal. My daddy was so smart! He taught other inmates how to read, write, and do math. He would send me spelling words through the mail. We would have to go over the words when he called. As a kid, I'd be so proud to get them all right when he called later in the week.

Before he passed, he told me, "I'm glad you're going into ministry. I wish I knew my calling." That broke me. If I knew then what I know now, I would've told him—"Dad, your calling was how you taught, how you cared. You kept fighting, even when life hurt you. Still, you wanted people to learn."

He never became the grandfather I knew he could've been. 2010 will always be the year I wish we could erase. I never got to ask him all my questions—about his childhood, his pain, or why he stayed connected to the wrong people. But one thing I know for sure: he loved his four children and grandchildren.

We love you FOREVER, Pops!

| 4 |

My Baby, My Battle!

I was two months pregnant when I told the father of my child, "I'm expecting." His response:
"It's not my baby!"

This is where I believe I absorbed the burden of shame—and it didn't arrive alone. It brought fear, rejection, insecurity, and silence. I became one of "them." You know, the girl murmured about in church hallways and school bathrooms. The one from whom little was ever expected.

The nerve of this boy, and his response! Shame settled on my lap as if invited. Hadn't I carried enough shame already? Then, in that moment, I faced the truth: I was going to raise a baby alone. My son's father never gave me a reason for not being a father to Myron. I never asked, and even now, there's been no explanation. I don't know if he ever will. Eventually, I accepted that nothing would change, so I moved on. I had to.

Still, questions swirled: Who do I turn to now? Who guides me through my body's changes or helps pick out baby clothes? Who reassures me I'll be okay? Alone and afraid at sixteen and a half, I gave birth. Yes—Kisha, this is your baby, your battle. I was a child raising a child.

Confusion and overwhelm clouded my life's direction. It felt as if I were a complete failure. I disappointed my family and my church. Worst of all, I disappointed my younger self. In the midst of this pain, I cried out to God: "Why did You let this happen? Why me? Why now? This part of my life?" It was anything but easy.

Even though my mom, my grandmother, my aunts, and my cousins had all walked this road, my experience felt distinct. The weight was heavier. Wrestling with these feelings, I questioned why God had led me down the same path so many women in my family had already traveled. Only later did I realize—we rarely consider statistics until we become one.

Looking back now, I wish I had gone to therapy. I wish someone had encouraged me to process what I was losing. At sixteen, while I was gaining a son, I was losing the rest of my childhood. I never got to feel what it meant to be carefree or truly young. I had to grow up overnight, and I had to do it without the father of my child beside me. How do you care for someone else when you're still figuring out who you are?

I didn't know what life should look like now. I was living the life my mom tried to protect me from. Rejection had followed me always—my father hadn't been around, and now my child would feel the same ache and absence. When does this cycle end? How do I find peace with this path? I wanted to give up.

But then, on March 17, 1994, at 1:15 a.m., my son Myron was born. Suddenly, everything changed. In that moment, I saw beauty; I saw the purpose. Hope wrapped in a baby blanket materialized before me. My King had arrived. From that point on, I pressed "go" on my life, and determination became my fuel.

From that point forward, I had something—and someone—to fight for. Whether his dad showed up or not, I knew it was me and Myron against the world. That tunnel-vision mindset kicked in: my focus narrowed, and I grew confident in this fight. Uncertain about the future but sure of my love, I found the push I needed to move.

I still laugh at Dennisha saying I was Grandma Shirley's favorite—she wasn't wrong. As a grandmother myself, I get it. Back then, though, I carried a secret: a baby and a storm of shame. Walking in humiliation wasn't what I imagined. I thought his father and I were together. But once I got pregnant, he disappeared, and I began building walls.

Pain pushed me to a place of comfort. Settling became easier than healing. Even now, as I reflect, I still don't know why my son's father chose not to be involved. I've often asked myself if it was something I did. But let this be a public service announcement to everyone reading this, who may feel like it's your fault when you find yourself in a one-sided relationship:
You are not responsible for someone else's silence.
You're not responsible for how others respond to your truth.

I thank God I didn't let my thoughts destroy me. His absence could've caused me to neglect my child, but I loved Myron with everything in me. While other teen moms had support, I had to figure it out on my own. Only a few close friends knew my battle. Again, I wrestled with rejection, fear, and shame. But here's what I know now:
Shame doesn't win unless you let it.
Love is still stronger.
And your story, as well as my story, is still being written.

| 5 |

Depression-And What Does that Look Like

This is one of the hardest chapters for me to write because it's real, present, and close to home. Depression isn't always obvious. Sometimes it arrives as silence, sits at the dinner table as fatigue, or hides in short answers and missed calls.

My husband has battled depression since losing his father. Watching someone you love go through the pain of grief is heartbreaking. Trying to hold everything else together at the same time is even harder. Being an only child makes it even harder for him. He doesn't have siblings to share the emotional overload with. He has only me to help him.

That's where things get complicated. Marriage is a partnership—but being the "strong one" in tough times can feel isolating, as if I must set aside my own feelings to be the pillar and encourager. How do you offer strength when you're running low yourself?

I remember a church service we attended years ago. A prophet took my arms, wrapped them around my husband, and said, "Strength for the journey." We were young, broke, raising six children, and struggling. I thought her words were for that time. But in 2024, I realized they were meant for this season of cancer and loss—the challenge we didn't see coming.

The moment the call came, I'll never forget: "Big Kip has transitioned." I handed the phone to my husband. I couldn't bear to hear the words, but Kip spoke them out loud, almost in disbelief: "My father is dead." The grief in the room was heavy. Stillness. Shock. Painful.

That was our reality check.

Suddenly, we were forced to reimagine our future. How does life move forward without a man like Big Kip? For a son who had his father through every season of life—what does this new chapter look like? As his wife, I've asked myself: How do I walk with him through this valley of loss? I've experienced loss too. My father passed away in 2010. But I have siblings. I had people to lean on. Kip doesn't have that. He leans on me. The truth is—I'm tired.

Grief can be unpredictable, and depression adds another harder-to-see layer. For Kip, losing his father was more than an earth-shattering event—it uncovered a deeper struggle. It wasn't just sadness; it was a heaviness that stayed long after his father's passing. Some days it was fatigue that rest couldn't fix; other days, unexpected quietness. Depression often hides in how our minds and bodies react to pain and stress.

Kip's journey shows grief and depression are connected but distinct. Grief appeared in missing his dad; depression whispered that life had lost meaning. Healing required him to seek help, lean on faith, and be honest about his mental health. It's a reminder that healing is emotional, physical, spiritual, and chemical. Acknowledging depression in grief is vital—because one may fade while the other lingers. Both deserve compassion and care.

We fought against breast cancer. We fought against financial hardship. We have raised children through hard times and difficult changes. Now, another battle has arrived—unexpected and daunting. And I can't help but cry out to God, "Why this fight? Why now?"

But even as I ask, I hear the echo of the prophet's words: "Strength for the journey." Not the strength to fix everything. But the strength to stand. The strength to hold my husband, to uplift him in prayer, and hold him through those uncertain moments. The strength to still believe in God's plan when life feels like it's falling apart.

Remember, depression doesn't always show up as an emotional outburst. Sometimes it's a quiet withdrawal from the world. The numbness. The pain. I've learned I can't carry his pain for him. But I can walk beside him on his journey of healing. When he's lost for words, I can always pray. I can sit in silence when he doesn't want to talk, and simply be there, just to show that I see him. I believe in Kip's healing, even when it feels slow.

And most of all, I can trust that even in this—God is present. Even in this, He is still faithful.

| 6 |

Empty nesters-The Release of Children

For Kip and me, parenting has been both our greatest joy and most demanding mission. Raising six children, including two sets of twins, kept our home full of laughter, noise, challenges, prayers, and purpose. Our youngest twins will turn 24 in August. Realizing our children are now adults, whether living at home or on their own, has brought reflection—and, honestly, inner conflict.

This stage of life is often called "empty nesting," but for us, it feels more like fighting for a new identity. It's not just about a quiet house; it's about releasing, trusting, and redefining what family looks like now. Some of our children still live at home, while others have launched into adulthood. But no matter where they are physically or emotionally, they remain tethered to us. And that's where the fight begins.

The fight is on because letting go has many layers. We're not just releasing them into adulthood; we're releasing our need to be needed, as we once were. We're releasing control, daily routines, and even some of the dreams we put on hold while raising them. It's a fight against our own expectations of what this stage was "supposed" to look like.

Kip and I make time for ourselves. We travel, laugh, and enjoy each other without always thinking about our adult children. These moments are healing and necessary. But even on getaways or quiet dinners, we still wonder: How are the kids? Do they need us? Are they okay? Sometimes, the house is too quiet, and we miss the footsteps, late-night fridge raids, and requests for rides or advice. Other times, when adult children and grandchildren return, the house is full—with their personalities, decisions, and sometimes conflict. We ask: How do we support without smothering, love without overstepping, and make room for their growth while allowing ours?

Kip and I have had late-night conversations, laughing and crying, about what this phase means. We've wrestled with guilt—should we have done more, or less? We've felt deep pride watching our children enter adulthood, yet the ache of release remains. Why is this a fight? Because love doesn't let go easily.

Parenting shaped our identities for decades, and letting go means redefining not only who they are but who we are. We're not just Mom and Dad anymore—we're two people relearning how to hold hands, dream, rest, and let our children rise, stumble, and find their own way. This isn't a fight against them; it's within us. It's a sacred struggle to trust God, believe what we've poured in will bear fruit, and find joy in what is and what's to come.

Before ending this chapter, I want to prepare your heart for what comes next. In the pages ahead, you will meet three women I love: my Aunt Monalisa, my cousin Dennisha, and my best friend Erica. Each walked a road no mother dreams of.
Aunt Monalisa lost her son, Jermaine, to gun violence. Gun violence also took Dennisha's son, Kevin. Domestic violence claimed Erica's son, Lil Marvin.

Their stories are raw and full of love for their sons—painful yet powerful testimonies of faith, survival, and strength. I invite you to walk with them, to listen, to feel, and see how God met them in their darkest moments.

| 7 |

Aunt Monalisa's Story

I want to share my story with the world. My son Jermaine left this world in 2008. After that, I honestly didn't know how to make it through each day. His passing from gun violence shattered my reality. It left a void that nothing could fill. For a long time, I couldn't accept that he was truly gone. It wasn't until 2013 or 2014 that I began to face the truth. There was an indescribable heaviness in my heart. Even now, over a decade later, the pain remains. It's a constant reminder of a loss both unbearable and surreal.

Jermaine was my firstborn twin, born on April 12, 1984, a day of immense joy. Holding him and his brother, Jermare, I felt a love that changed my world. Jermaine's gentle spirit, protective nature, and calm assurance made him incredibly special. I often reminisce about his smile and the peaceful way he approached life, feeling immense pride in the young man he was and the dreams I had for his future.

There are moments when I sit with the reality that if I had lost Jermaine when he was younger, I don't think I would have made it. Although he became a grown man by 2008, I found some strength, and though his life was cut short, it was full. Still, the pain runs deep. I try my best to hide my grief from my other children because I don't want to pass my sadness onto them. I want to keep positive energy around them, even when I'm hurting inside. I silence my grief by going into my room, closing the door, and letting the tears fall. That's my quiet space, where I let the pain speak freely.

Even now, there are parts of this journey I still struggle with. One of the hardest things is visiting his gravesite. I've never found peace there. Every time I think about going, a heavyweight settles on my heart. It brings a wave of pain that's hard to bear—it makes it feel too final. I know he's not there in spirit, but standing there makes the loss feel fresh. So, I carry him with me in my thoughts, memories, prayers, and every time I speak his name.

Something bittersweet happened just weeks after Jermaine passed in 2008. My first grandson, Ashton, was born on March 23, 2008—just 21 days after Jermaine departed this life on March 2. Though I was grieving deeply, Ashton's birth brought a flicker of light into my darkness. It felt like I had my three sons all over again. Holding Ashton reminded me of Jermaine in the most beautiful way. It was as if God sent a piece of him back to me, a quiet reminder that life continues, even amid the pain.

Every day I carry the weight of his absence, yet I am sustained by the memory of his laughter and our love. Because his spirit gives me strength, I honor his life by keeping his memory alive. In telling my story, I seek healing and hope to let others know that even in loss, love continues. His life mattered, and sharing that truth helps me breathe a little easier, one day at a time.

| 8 |

Dennisha's Story

Losing Kevin broke me in a way I don't think I'll ever fully recover from. He was murdered in D.C. in July 2021, and from that day forward, life just hasn't felt the same. I share Kevin's story to honor his memory and fight for change so others don't suffer as we have. Kevin was my second child, my loud one, my funny one, my heart in so many ways.

His big, beautiful smile could light up a room, and I miss it every single day. When he laughed, so did everyone around him. Even his silliest jokes would make us crack up. Kevin loved making people laugh—through his hilarious videos or just by being his goofy self. That joy he shared defined him.

Though he didn't have kids of his own, he poured so much love into his brothers and sisters. With eight of them together, his presence always filled the house. Now, his absence leaves a quiet that sometimes feels overwhelming, reminding us all just how much life he brought to our home.

Kevin loved Thanksgiving. It was his favorite time of year—he talked about it weeks ahead. He loved the food, family, and the noise when we were all together. I can still picture him piling his plate high, joking, dancing in the kitchen, making us laugh until our sides hurt. Now, on that day, there's a hole we all feel. His seat is empty, and it just hurts.

I think about everything he didn't get to do. He had plans, dreams, and so much life in him. He should've had the chance to grow older, to have kids, to live. But someone took that from him. Taken from all of us.

That hurt is the reason I fight—in Kevin's memory, for the joy he brought, and for every mother facing this pain. Kevin wasn't just a number or a story in the news; he was my son, full of light, laughter, and love. I'll keep saying his name and telling his story because he mattered, and he still does.

To every mother who's faced this loss—who's said goodbye too soon—I want you to know: I see you. I carry your pain because I live it each day. Yet, I believe you can keep going. The pain doesn't fade, but God gives strength, one moment at a time. When it feels impossible, trust Him. Cry if you need. Scream if you must. But keep moving forward. Even in heartbreak, God remains near. He's still faithful.

You are not alone. We keep fighting, side by side. Even in the darkness, we trust that God is writing something greater than we can see right now.

| 9 |

Erica's Story

March 5th, 1990, was a day that changed my life forever; my first child, Marvin, was born. However, on July 3rd, 2013, my life changed in a way that I feel I will never recover from. I lost my son that day, which devastated me. Not only did I lose my child, but that date was two days before my birthday, which I never felt the same about again.

The person who took my son's life was someone whom I thought of as a daughter and who had been around my family for years. Sometime before the incident, my son persuaded my daughter and me to let this person live with us. By the time of the incident, she was still living with my daughter, even though she and my son were no longer together and had moved on to other relationships. At that point, my son was splitting his time between his girlfriend's home and his father's home. Once their relationship became volatile, he decided to move out so she could have a place to live.

On the day that changed everything, I was at work. I stepped away from my desk for just a couple of minutes. Upon returning, I discovered a missed call from my son's father around 2 pm. It wasn't until I checked his voicemail that the gravity of the moment hit me.

He was yelling, saying that I needed to call him because she had stabbed our son, who was in the ambulance on the way to the hospital. I called him to get more information, but that was all he knew, since he was at work when I called.

As I was on my way to the hospital, a feeling came over me, and I knew my son was gone.

I arrived at the hospital. We were told to wait because the police wanted to speak to us. I didn't want to talk to anyone—just to see my son one last time. Fifteen minutes later, they escorted us to another room. Three doctors came in and gave us the worst news of my life. It felt unreal until I saw his father go from praying to collapsing in tears. My significant other held me as I sobbed. He asked if he should pick up my other two children so I could tell them. I agreed, though I wasn't sure how I would do it.

He left to get them, and though he returned quickly, I later learned he had to pull over and call his parents for support after becoming overwhelmed with emotion while picking up the children. By the time they arrived at the hospital, I had spent as much time as allowed with my son, who was now lying there with tubes, a sheet pulled up to his neck, and his body growing cold. All I could do in those moments was hold him tight, trying to warm him and telling him how much he meant to me and how much I loved him.

I came out of the room and saw my other two children crying. That's when I knew someone had already told them. I walked over and held them tightly. I tried to make them feel at ease, like I always have when they were younger. It broke me when my youngest told me he felt like a part of him was gone. He doesn't know what to do. My response was that we're going to continue to love, talk, and live as though he's standing right next to us.

Another thing that happened that day was that, as we were leaving for the hospital, my dad and stepmother were on their way back. When my dad saw how upset we were, he broke down and cried—a rare occurrence, as I had only seen him cry once before when my mother passed away. The ride home after the hospital was quiet; I stared out the window into the sky, hoping this was all just a bad dream, but deep down I knew it wasn't.

Once I arrived home, everyone from the neighborhood was offering their condolences. His friends were coming, and my house became so busy that I had to stop accepting visitors so I could process what had happened. My mindset was to make sure my other children would be okay. I wanted to make sure my firstborn would rest peacefully.

The celebration of life for my son was so amazing—full of love, people, and stories about the many lives he had touched. Regarding the person responsible, she did not receive any jail time. Instead, she was sentenced to attend treatment at Saint Elizabeth Hospital a couple of days a week, with the condition that missing treatment would result in jail. I was furious with this decision, but I was told her own life had been full of trauma and that she hadn't been taking her medication when the incident happened. I never knew she was on medication. My focus remained on my other children and how they would process such a loss.

Months later, when I unexpectedly saw this person again, I could only hug her and cry. Only two people know about that encounter; not even my children. I don't believe my response would be the same if I saw her again, but so far, I haven't.

I truly thank God for my strength, for making me a fighter, and for helping me process and deal with all the trials and tribulations I have endured throughout my life.

I would also like to thank my significant other and best friend, who is more like a sister, for being there for me through many tough times. I appreciate them with all my heart, and I thank GOD for placing these two individuals in my life.

———————————

After reading Erica's story about her son Marvin, it's clear that life's battles can sometimes feel unbearable. Stories like hers, my Aunt Mona's, and my cousin Dennisha remind us that pain is real. Grief is real, and the weight of loss can sit heavily on our hearts. But they also remind us of something greater. Even in the darkest valleys, God is still present, and His purpose can still shine through.

This is why I want to leave you with something encouraging as we move into the last chapter of this book. The title may sound heavy—The Purpose of This Fight—but I assure you, it is not an ending of sorrow. It is a declaration of victory. Everything you have read up until now, every testimony of pain and struggle, has pointed to one truth: there is purpose in every battle we face.

So, as you turn the page, be encouraged. The fight may be hard, but it is never wasted. God always has a purpose. In the next chapter, we will discover together the purpose of this fight.

Now, let's turn the page…

| 10 |

The Purpose of THIS fight

We don't always get to choose the fight. But God always chooses us for it. If He allows it, there is a purpose in it. "This" fight—whatever yours may be—is not a chastisement. It is preparation. It's a process. It's personal.

When I say 'this fight', I'm talking about the current one you may be in. You may not have shared it with anyone. Internal battles are the ones that can overtake you. The one that keeps you up at night. The one you wrestle with in your mind, in your spirit, and sometimes in silence. For my husband, Kip, and me, we've had different fights—parenting, health challenges, grief, transition, identity, marriage, finances, and even the quiet fight to remain faithful when things weren't moving fast enough. But what we've learned is that God does not waste a single battle. Not one.

There is a unique assignment in the fight God allows you to face. Your fight may not look like mine: perhaps you aren't raising six children, recovering from breast cancer, or rediscovering yourself as an empty nester. Even so, you are likely facing something that tests your strength. Remember, you are not alone. It is okay to be tired; you are not weak. You're not faithless for being confused. You're simply in a fight—a fight that God has already gone before you and conquered.

We often think strength is about pretending like nothing's wrong. However, I learned that true strength is surrendering to the process and trusting that there is a purpose in what's painful. To underscore this, the Bible tells us in Romans 8:28 that "all things work together for the good for them who love God and are called according to His purpose." This reveals that even your storm is part of God's strategy. Your tears will water something that blooms in another season. It means your pressure is producing perseverance. This fight is not in vain.

Some fights teach you how to wait. Some teach you how to walk away. Others teach you to wage war in prayer. This fight may push you deeper into who you are in Christ—not just who you've had to be for others. This fight may strip away pride, false identities, and control, but it will clothe you with purpose if you allow it.

Kip and I have had to lean into each other and lean into God during some of our hardest fights. But it was in those moments that we saw His faithfulness most clearly. When our plans fell apart, God's purpose still stood. And sometimes, that's the point of the fight—to show us we were never in control to begin with. His strength becomes perfect in our weakness. We don't need to have all the answers—we just need to trust the one who does.

So, why this fight?

This fight is building your character. Your prayers are being manifested. This is the one that is humbling you, shaping you, and making your heart tender again. This is the one that may finally break what needs to be broken so God can rebuild it His way. You didn't choose it, but you are still chosen for it. You may not understand the why yet, but I encourage you to ask God, "What are You trying to show me in this?" Because the moment you shift from why me to Yes, Lord? — is the moment purpose rises from the pain.

Every story in this book has carried its own measure of pain; some have been heavy, some silent and hidden. But one truth remains: pain is not the end of the story. Pain may break us, but it also builds us. It refines and prepares us for something greater.

The fight was never just about us.

It's about those we will help, the ones who find strength in our stories. It's proof that, even in the darkest valley, God walks with us and never lets the fight destroy what He designed us to become. I've come to understand that the battles I wanted to escape were the ones shaping me for my calling. The tears I cried watered the seeds of resilience. The losses I suffered taught me how to value what truly matters. And every time I thought the fight would take me out, God was actually lifting me up.

If you're carrying battles of your own, let this be your reminder: your fight is not wasted. There is purpose in your struggle. There is victory on the other side of your tears. Don't give up. Don't let the weight of your fight convince you it's meaningless. Stand tall, even when it hurts. Because the day will come when you look back and say, This fight gave me strength, clarity, and purpose.

And when that day does come, you'll know — the fight was never meant to destroy you. It was meant to reveal you. So keep pressing on, embrace the journey, and let your story inspire others. Your next step forward is the start of something powerful.

www.ingramcontent.com/pod-product-compliance
Lightning Source LLC
Chambersburg PA
CBHW071228130626
46555CB00004B/1889